Roman Schmidt

Discount Certificates
An Alternative to Stock Investments

Diplomica® Verlag GmbH

**Schmidt, Roman: Discount Certificates: An Alternative to Stock Investments,
Hamburg, Diplomica Verlag GmbH 2011**
Originaltitel der Studienarbeit: Discount Certificates: An Alternative to Stock Investments

ISBN: 978-3-86341-062-9
Druck Diplomica® Verlag GmbH, Hamburg, 2011
Zugl. FOM - Fachhochschule für Oekonomie und Management Essen, Essen,
Deutschland, Studienarbeit , 2010

Bibliografische Information der Deutschen Nationalbibliothek:
Die Deutsche Nationalbibliothek verzeichnet diese Publikation in der Deutschen
Nationalbibliografie;
detaillierte bibliografische Daten sind im Internet über http://dnb.d-nb.de abrufbar.

Die digitale Ausgabe (eBook-Ausgabe) dieses Titels trägt die ISBN 978-3-86341-562-4
und kann über den Handel oder den Verlag bezogen werden.

Dieses Werk ist urheberrechtlich geschützt. Die dadurch begründeten Rechte, insbesondere die der Übersetzung, des Nachdrucks, des Vortrags, der Entnahme von Abbildungen und Tabellen, der Funksendung, der Mikroverfilmung oder der Vervielfältigung auf anderen Wegen und der Speicherung in Datenverarbeitungsanlagen, bleiben, auch bei nur auszugsweiser Verwertung, vorbehalten. Eine Vervielfältigung dieses Werkes oder von Teilen dieses Werkes ist auch im Einzelfall nur in den Grenzen der gesetzlichen Bestimmungen des Urheberrechtsgesetzes der Bundesrepublik Deutschland in der jeweils geltenden Fassung zulässig. Sie ist grundsätzlich vergütungspflichtig. Zuwiderhandlungen unterliegen den Strafbestimmungen des Urheberrechtes.

Die Wiedergabe von Gebrauchsnamen, Handelsnamen, Warenbezeichnungen usw. in diesem Werk berechtigt auch ohne besondere Kennzeichnung nicht zu der Annahme, dass solche Namen im Sinne der Warenzeichen- und Markenschutz-Gesetzgebung als frei zu betrachten wären und daher von jedermann benutzt werden dürften.

Die Informationen in diesem Werk wurden mit Sorgfalt erarbeitet. Dennoch können Fehler nicht vollständig ausgeschlossen werden, und die Diplomarbeiten Agentur, die Autoren oder Übersetzer übernehmen keine juristische Verantwortung oder irgendeine Haftung für evtl. verbliebene fehlerhafte Angaben und deren Folgen.

© Diplomica Verlag GmbH
http://www.diplom.de, Hamburg 2011
Printed in Germany

Executive Summary

This work evaluates investments in discount certificates as an alternative to stock investments.

It gives general information on the construction of discount certificates and their markets.

In Addition, it describes and compares the opportunities and risks of stock investments and investments in discount certificates. It evaluates the development in value of both investments in different market environments. Using a fictive example, it shows that discount certificates outperform stocks in most market situations.

The paper provides strategies for investments in discount certificates and evaluates them.

TABLE OF CONTENTS

List of Abbreviations 8

List of Figures 8

List of Tables 8

1   Introduction 9

2   The Discount Certificate 11
2.1   Definition and General Information 11
2.2   Markets for Discount Certificates 12

3   Differentiation of Discount Certificates and stocks 15
3.1   Opportunities and risks 15
3.2   Evaluation 18

4   Behavior of Discount Certificates in Different Market Scenarios 19
4.1   Assumptions 19
4.2   Five Market Scenarios 20
4.2.1   The Growth Scenario 20
4.2.2   The Moderate Growth Scenarios 22
4.2.3   The Stagnation Scenario 24
4.2.4   The Moderate Decline Scenarios 26
4.2.5   The Decline Scenario 28
4.3   Special considerations when investing in discount certificates 30
4.4   Evaluation and Critical Review 31

5   Strategies for investing into Discount Certificates 33
5.1   Classic Strategies 33

5.2 Unconventional Strategies 34
5.2.1 The short maturity strategy 35
5.2.1.1 The short maturity strategy combined with the offensive investment strategy 35
5.2.1.2 The short maturity strategy combined with the neutral strategy 36
5.2.1.3 The short maturity strategy combined with the defensive strategy 36
5.2.2 The low volatility strategy 37

6 Conclusion 39

Reference List 41

LIST OF ABBREVIATIONS

EUWAX   European Warrant Exchange (Stuttgart)

DC   discount certificate

OTC   over-the-counter (-trading)

LIST OF FIGURES

Figure 1: Growth 21
Figure 2: Growth I 22
Figure 3: Moderate Growth II 23
Figure 4: Stagnation I 25
Figure 5: Stagnation II 26
Figure 6: Moderate Decline I 27
Figure 7: Moderate Decline II 28
Figure 8: Decline 29

LIST OF TABLES

Table 1: List of Variables 20
Table 2: Payout Growth 21
Table 3: Payout Moderate Growth I 23
Table 4: Payout Moderate Growth II 24
Table 5: Payout Stagnation I 25
Table 6: Payout Stagnation II 26
Table 7: Payout Moderate Decline I 27
Table 8: Payout Moderate Decline II 28
Table 9: Payout Decline 30

1 Introduction

In 1985 Thomas Zwirner of HSBC Trinkaus invented the Discount Certificate by copying an investment strategy of professional investors (Schmidt 2008).

Now there are over 100,000 certificates traded on the European Warrant Exchange (EUWAX). About 80% are discount certificates (Boerse Stuttgart AG 2010). Many Banks promote discount certificates as a safer and more profitable investment than a direct investment in stocks. However, when Lehman Brothers has filed bankruptcy in 2008 many investors lost their money invested in Lehman certificates (London Stock Exchange plc. 2008). Investors may now ask themselves the question if certificates and especially discount certificates are a true alternative to a stock investment.

The following work will answer this question. It is structured as follows: Chapter 2 describes basic information about discount certificates; it also provides information on the markets for discount certificates. Chapter 3 will identify and evaluate the risks and opportunities of a direct stock investment and a investment in discount certificates. Chapter 4 evaluates the behavior of discount certificates and stocks in different market scenarios by using a fictive example.

In chapter 5 possible strategies for an investment in discount certificates are given by the author and evaluated on their risk and opportunities, while chapter 6 concludes.

Since there are many different types of discount certificates, this work will focus on the discount certificates with an underlying of one share of the respective company.

2 The Discount Certificate

2.1 Definition and General Information

A Discount Certificate (DC) is a financial product, which is set up by banks and sold to private and institutional investors. The structure of a DC locates it in the product family called derivatives. A Derivative is "a contract that derives most of its value from some underlying asset, reference rate, or index" (Kolb, Overdahl 2003). A DC has usually on share of the respective company as an underlying.

A DC is a contract between the investor and the issuing bank which allows the investor to participate in the value development of an underlying stock with a lower initial investment than investing directly into the underlying. In the legal perspective this resembles an unsecured bond. The participation is limited in time – maturity (Commerzbank AG 2009). There is, however, no call for additional cover implied by investing in DCs.

The discount acts like an airbag, which decreases the loss of an investment if the underlying decreases in value and increases the profit, which the investor makes if the underlying increases in value.

However, every advantage comes with a price. In the case of the DC the price for the discount is called cap. The cap resembles a barrier which limits the participation in value development and thereby limiting the maximum profit for the investor.

A DC consists of a zero-strike-call and a sold call-option (short call). The zero-strike-call is a call-option for the underlying with a base price of zero. It represents the price of the underlying excluding the anticipated dividends paid within its maturity. With buying a DC the investor indirectly sells a call-option for the underlying. The value of the DC is the price of the zero-strike-bond less the value of the call-option. The base price of the call-option represents the cap of the DC (Maaß 2007). The DC changes its value according to the change of these two components in different market environments (Chapter 4). The level of the cap compared to the price of the underlying, the maturity of the DC, and the implicit volatility of the underlying influence the price of the DC as well. The time of maturity is determined by the maturity of the zero-strike-call and the maturity of the short call. During the maturity the DC does not pay dividends like a stock. The profit of the investor is only determined by the increase in value. When the DC matures it will have the value of the zero-strike-call.

The DC has two payout possibilities. If the underlying notes above or on the cap, the investor will receive the value of the cap in cash. If the underlying notes below the cap he[1] will receive the stock.

2.2 Markets for Discount Certificates

DCs are traded on the primary and the secondary market (Alexander, Sheedy 2008 p. 111). The primary market describes the first offering of a stock (initial public offering) or another financial product (e. g. DC). "The secondary market consists of the buying and selling of already issued [financial products]" (Alexander, Sheedy 2008 p.113).

The secondary market for DCs can be divided into an unregulated market (over-the-counter-trading) and a regulated market (stock exchange).

On the primary market the issuer sells a fixed number of DCs to investors. This selling process takes place in a limited time span. The investor does not have to pay stock market fees and is able to participate in gaining of the DC immediately. However, some conditions of the DC sold, may be fixed after the investors has purchased them. Some issuers will also charge an issuing fee undo the advantage of not paying stock market fees. (Brechmann, Röder et al. 2008 p. 75-76)

All further buys and sales take place in the secondary market. There are always to prices quoted on the secondary market. The difference between the price of buying and selling a DC is called spread and resembles the profit margin of the trading partner in the secondary market.

A DC can be traded over-the-counter (OTC). In an OTC-trade the investor conducts the transaction directly with the issuer of the DC by cutting out the middle man (exchange). One advantage for an investor in trading OTC is the extension of trading hours, which enables the investor to buy or sell DCs even if the stock market is

---

[1] Femals are always included.

closed. Another advantages is the smaller cost of transaction, since the investors has not to pay any stock market fees.

There are two exchanges in Germany which have specialist in certificate investing – EUWAX (Stuttgart) and Scoach (Frankfurt). Both exchanges offer the investor the regulatory measures including the best-price-principle, miss-trade-rules, and a limit-control-system. The first ensures that a transaction is conducted at the best price within the spread. The second defines what a miss-trade is and how to reverse it. The last measure ensures that an order placed by an investor is executable (Brechmann, Röder et al. 2008 p. 76 – 77). However, the investor has to pay this security by paying a market fee. Although the exchange is designed to bring bids and asks of private investors together, the extreme high number of DCs traded makes it very improbable that to investors will pair in a trade. For that reason the stock market requires the issuers of DCs to act as market makers constantly prompting bids and asks quotes. An investor will most certainly have the issuer of the DC as a trading partner in the warrant exchange (Baule, Entrop et al. 2008 p1). This results in the dangerous position for the investor. He is dependable on one counterpart in the trading. This limits the advantages of a stock exchange and introduces risks to a DC investor which are further discussed in chapter 3.2.

3 Differentiation of Discount Certificates and stocks

3.1 Opportunities and risks

DCs and stocks expose the investor to certain opportunities and risks. Since the DC is derived from the stock (underlying), some are similar. However, there are certain opportunities and risks, which apply only to the DC.

A stock investment offers two ways of making a profit. The first is appreciation. An investor can buy a stock at a certain price and sell it at a much higher value. The difference resembles the profit. The second is dividends paid. A stock owner is entitled to a share of the profit of the particular company of which he owns the stock. If the company is profitable the investor receives a certain amount of money every year - called dividends. Stock investments also give voting rights to investors, which enables them to influence the company's way of doing business.

As mentioned in Chapter 2.1 the DC does not pay dividends. So the only way of making a profit is selling the DC back to the issuer at a higher price than the investor has bought it. The sale either happens automatically when the DC matures, or during the maturity (Chapter 2.2).
The issuer sells the DC at a discount, which enables to investor to buy the underlying stock at a smaller price. At the end of the maturity the value of the DC equals the value of the stock or cap. So the investor posses the chance to make a profit even if the underlying stock does not performs in a positive way. The discount adds to profit in a positive market scenario. In addition, the investor can use the saved money to buy other investment products, e. g. DCs with a different underlying stock.
Chapter 4 describes the situations in which a DC is more profitable than a direct stock investment.

The economic risk refers to the "risk associated with the overall health of the economy in the locality the investment is made" (Federal Reserve Bank of Atlanta 2009).

For a stock investor the economic risk consists only of the uncertainty about the development of the economy the respective company is located in. If the company performs poorly the value of the underlying stock drops resulting in a loss for the investor (Chapter 5.1). In Addition, expected dividends may not be paid.

The same is true for a person investing in DCs. In addition, the investor interested in buying a DC has to consider the health of the economy in which the issuer operates in. DCs are unsecured bonds. This legal characteristic exposes the investor to the credit default risk. The investor may realize a total loss of his money invested in DCs irrespective to the performance of the underlying. If the issuer of the DCs files bankruptcy, the investor will only be entitled to a small compensation according to value of the issuer after it has been liquidated. The default of Lehman Brothers in 2008 is a prominent example for this risk. (Commerzbank AG 2009 p. 4)

The foreign currency risk describes the risk implied by a change of the exchange rate between two currencies (Organisation for Economic Co-operation and Development [OECD] 2005 p.132). If the investor (located in the Eurozone) buys a stock or other financial product in another currency e.g. Dollar, then the value of the investment can change only due to a change in the exchange rate. If the Dollar decreases in value compared to the Euro, the investor makes a lost on his investment even if the nominal value of the financial product has not changed. A person invested in DCs with an underlying of stocks denominated in a foreign currency, Is exposed to the same risk. However the mechanism works in both directions, therefore an investor may use a current weakness of the foreign currency to buy DCs. The currency exchange rate will then work as leverage for the investment. The same chance is also implied in an investment in stocks (denominated in a foreign currency).

An investor interested in DCs faces the problem that the issuer of a DC may quote unfavourable prices. As explained in Chapter 2.2 the issuer of a DC is virtually involved in every transaction of a DC. Wilkens, Erner, and Röder (2003) describe the order flow hypothesis which states that the issuer of a DC orientates the pricing of a DC in accordance to the life cycle of the product. The issuer does not quote a fair price of the DC, but a price according to the risk of redeeming the DC in stocks. As a consequence the price of a DC differs more from the fair price the longer the maturity time is (p. 2 and p. 24-25).

In addition, Baule, Entrop, and Wilkens (2008) point out, that the position as a market maker enables the issuer to realize a margin higher, which is higher than the margin of the components of a DC. The investor is in danger of being put into a disadvantageous position by the market power of the issuing institute (p. 1 and 2).

The fair value of the DC is also determined by its legal structure (Chapter 2.1). The issuer incorporates "its own risk in the payoff structure" (Baule, Entrop et al. 2008 p. 2).

However, for an investor it is also necessary to evaluate the value of a DC not only through evaluating its components, but also to take the transaction costs of reproducing the DC in consideration. Depending on the structure of a DC the transaction costs of buying the single components of a DC individually may exceed the disadvantages in the pricing of a DC by the issuer.

The investor, therefore, has always to consider the both aspects when thinking about investing in DCs. Although the pricing of a DC may be disadvantageous compared to its components, it may still be a better deal than buying them individually (e. g. when considering transaction costs).

An investor in stocks participates in the profit of the respective company by payments of dividends. A DC does not pay dividends. So the only way for the investor to make profit with the DC is by selling it at higher price than he purchased it. If the investor holds the DC until maturity, he will risk to have made less profit than investing directly into a stock. This situation occurs, when the combined profit of value increase and dividends of the stock exceeds the increase in value of the discount certificate including the discount.

In Addition, a change in the expected dividends paid also influences the price of the DC during the time of maturity. If the amount of dividends paid increases the value of the zero-strike-call drops, thereby decreasing the value of the DC. So an increase of dividends may result in a loss for an investor planning to sell the DC before it matures.

The tradability of DCs represents a special risk to potential investors. As described in chapter 2.2, the issuer is virtually the only the only possible trading partner for an investor of DCs.

However an issuer may decide any time to stop taking the role as a trading partner. It can stop quoting bids and asks at the stock market at any point. The OTC-trading may be stopped due to a change in business policies or a lack of liquidity of the issuing institution. An example for such an incident is provided by Commerzbank which declard that it would not act as a market maker for several certificates with an US-bank-share as underlying during the days of the Lehman Brothers bankruptcy. (Mohr 2008)

By investing into DCs the investor has realize that he risks holding illiquid assets. Although a stock may become harder to trade as a company performs very ill or has to file bankruptcy. The stock investor will have always the advantage of having more than one potential trading partner. This reduces the risk of not being able to cash in (even at a low price) when needed.

3.2 Evaluation

An investor faces opportunities and risks when investing in DCs and stocks. It is always important to evaluate both. However, as preceding chapters have shown, the most important risk (issuer's default risk) of DCs is imminent only in extreme market situations, e.g. a financial crisis. Although the other risks should not be neglected, they are offset in the opportunity of making profits during negative stock market scenarios. Chapter 4 gives a more detailed look at how DCs outperform stocks in different market scenarios and in which stocks are the superior choice of investment.

4 Behavior of Discount Certificates in Different Market Scenarios

4.1 Assumptions

The advantage of a DC over a stock investment is determined by the market development of the particular underlying stock. As in chapter 2.1 described the value of a DC is dependable on the value of each component. The following describes the development of value of a DC compared to an investment into the respective stock (underlying) in different market situations.

While most issuers of DC use a display showing the value of a DC in dependency to the stock, this sort of diagram is not sufficient to compare the value of an investment referring to the time span the money is invested. Therefore, the following figures show the value of a stock and a DC in depending on the time period the investment is maintained.

For the comparison of DCs and stock investments the following is assumed:
The investor has the choice to either invest into the stock of the sample company xyz or to purchase a DC with the stock of the company as the underlying. The investor will hold both investments for the maturity time of the DC.

There is no currency risk and the DC/stock can be traded on the spot at time of maturity. The company does not pay dividends on the stock. There are no transaction costs. If the DC converts to stock at the point of maturity it is sold immediately.

The following table explains the variables used in the examples:

Table 1: List of Variables

t_0	point in time of initial investment	$D_{1/2}$	value of the DC at $t_{1/2}$
t_1	point in time during the investment (specified in the example)	S_0	initial value of the stock
t_2	point in time of maturity/stock disposition	$S_{1/2}$	value of the stock at $t_{1/2}$
t_2-t_0	time frame of maturity	c	cap of the DC
D_0	initial value of the DC (S_0-d)	d	discount (S_0-D_0)

The charts in the following section are not true to scale, they serve visualization purposes only.

4.2 Five Market Scenarios

There are five possible market scenarios, which can occur. They can be described as growth, moderate growth, stagnation, moderate decline, and decline. While the growth scenario and the decline scenario have just one possible outcome for a DC investment, the other three have two outcomes.

4.2.1 The Growth Scenario

The first scenario describes a strong market environment in which an increase of value of the underlying is expected. In figure 1 the current stock value is $S_0=100$ and the value of the DC is D_0, which is 95. The cap of the DC has been set up to be c = 120.

The discount d is 5 points. The covered time period is t_2-t_0 with the DC maturing at t_2. Due to a strong market and good performance of the company xyz its stock (underlying) increases in value.

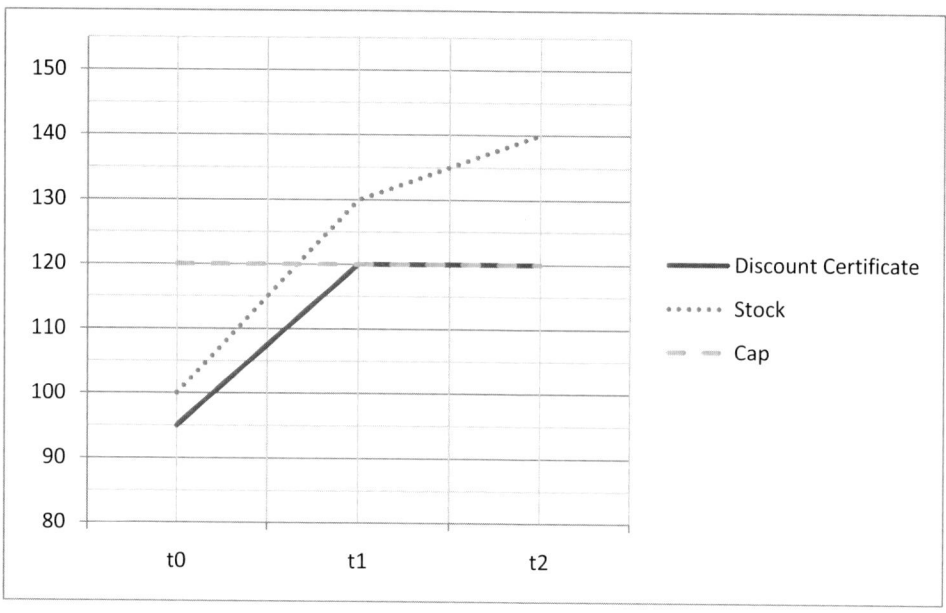

Figure 1: Growth

The value of the stock exceeds the cap of the DC within the time span of t_1-t_0. At t_1 the DC has reached its maximum value of 120 (cap). Although the value of the underlying increases further in the time period t_2-t_1, the DC does not increase its value to more than the cap value of 120.

In the given example, the stock price has increased to 140 at the time of maturity of the DC. If the investor now sells the stock he makes a greater profit than an investor who has bought the DC.

Table 2 shows the initial investment and the payout of the stock and the DC.

Table 2: Payout Growth

	Initial investment	payout	profit
DC	95	120	25 (26.3%)
stock	100	140	40 (40%)

An investor who expects a strong market growth in the future should not invest into DCs. A stock investment is more profitable.

4.2.2 The Moderate Growth Scenarios

In the second scenario the market environment has slightly chanced. In the following the investor still expects a positive development of the underlying stock. This time, however, the appreciation of the stock is not as strong as in the first scenario. The moderate increase in value makes two situations possible at the point of maturity. Either the underlying stock price quotes above the cap or below.

While the variables S_0, d and c stay the same as in the scenario above the stock increases only to S_2 (110) within the maturity time of the DC (t_2-t_0). This chart represents the situation when the stock price does not exceed the cap.

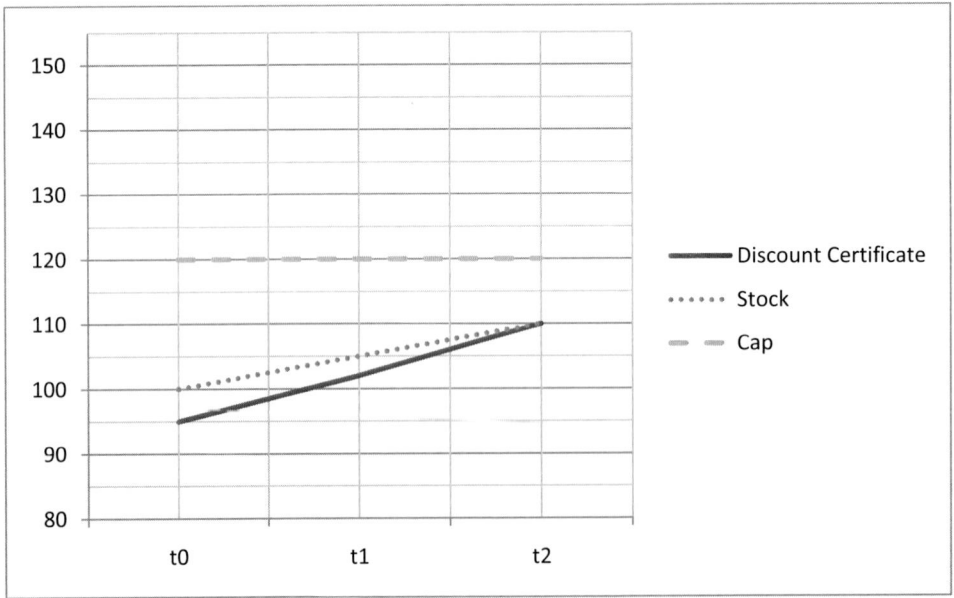

Figure 2: Growth I

As described in Chapter 2.1 the DC does not pay out cash if the cap is not reached or exceeded, instead the investors receives the share of the underlying stock. In consequence the investment into DCs will have the same value as the direct stock investment at t_2. Since the investor has received a discount compared to the stock value at the time buying the DC, he makes a greater profit than he would have made if he had invested directly into the stock.

Table 3: Payout Moderate Growth I

	Initial investment	payout	profit
DC	95	110	15 (15.8%)
stock	100	110	10 (10%)

In the second situation the stock price exceeds the cap. However, the accretion of the underlying has only been moderate.

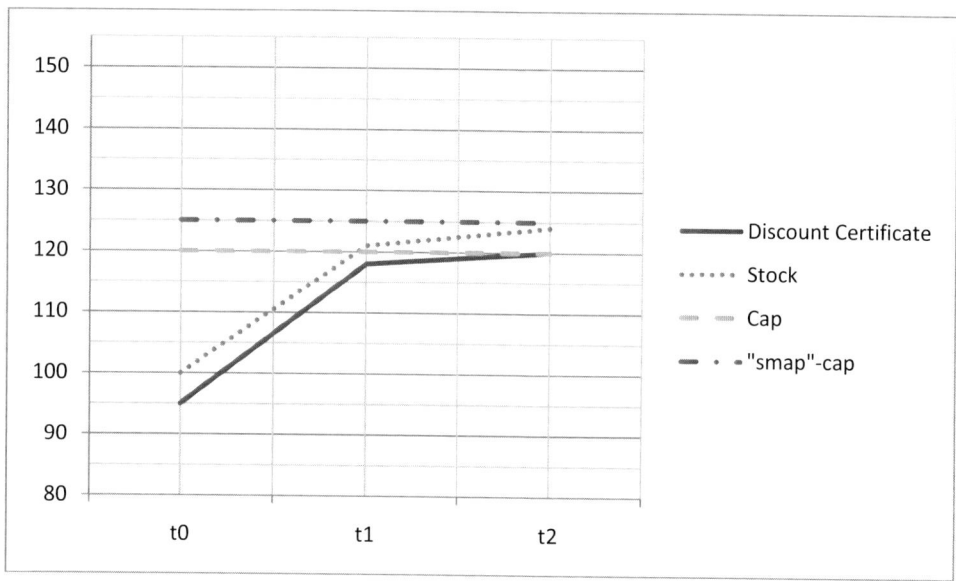

Figure 3: Moderate Growth II

In this case the DC investment generates a higher profit than a direct stock investment if at t_1 the value of the stock notes x higher than the cap for x < d.
This creates a second cap which can be called the "still-made-a-profit" cap. To calculate the "smap"-cap the following equation can be used:

smap-cap = c + d

The DC generates a profit at t_2 for:

$D_0 < S_2 < (c + d)$ and $c < S_2 < (c + d)$

For the example of company xyz the smap-cap is located at the share price of 125. Therefore an investor will make a greater profit with the investment in DCs than a direct stock investment if the cap is exceeded and the value of the underlying notes in the range of 120 to 125.

Table 4: Payout Moderate Growth II

	Initial investment	payout	profit
DC	95	120	25 (26.3%)
stock	100	120.1-124.9	20.1-24.9 (20.1% - 24.9%)

The profit is higher the closer the cap is chosen to the value of the stock at t_2. Expecting a moderate growth the DC investor is able to realize a greater profit than the stock investor.

4.2.3 The Stagnation Scenario

The stagnation in value of the underlying is characteristic for the third scenario. While all other variables stay the same, the stock price t_0 and t_2 is identical. So $S_0 = S_2$ is true.

To evaluate the profit an investor makes with a stock investment or a DC investment at the point in time t_2 it does not matter how good or bad the underlying or the DC performed in the time period t_2-t_0.

This scenario is only beneficial to the DC investor. While the stock does not experience an appreciation in the observed time span, the DC increases its value until it equals the stock value at the point of maturity (or the cap if the stock lists above it at maturity). There a two scenarios. The first is displayed in figure 4.

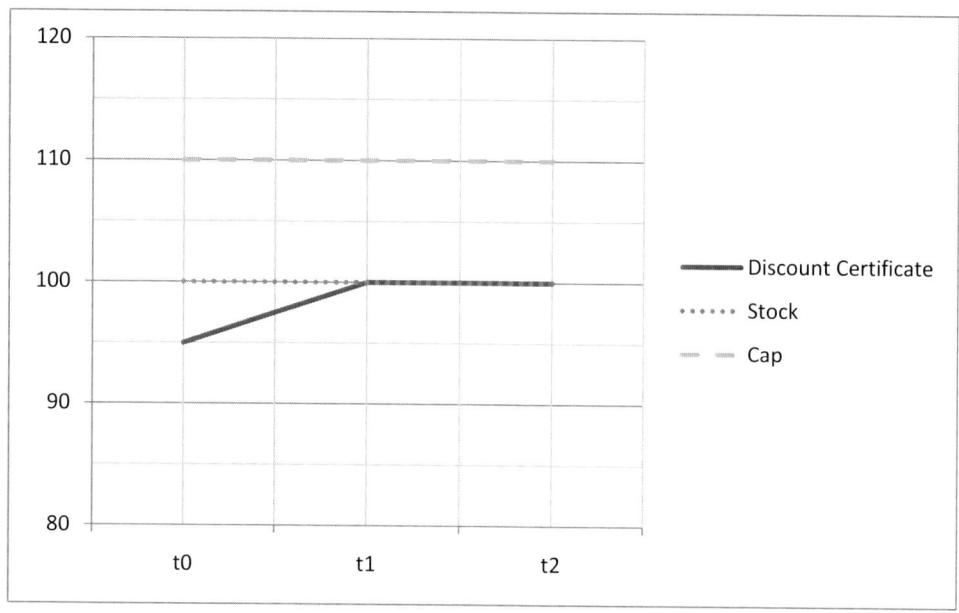

Figure 4: Stagnation I

The discount received at the time of purchasing the DC resembles the profit, if the stock notes under the cap at t_2.

Table 5: Payout Stagnation I

	Initial investment	payout	profit
DC	95	100	5 (5.3%)
stock	100	100	0 (0%)

If the cap is located below the value of the stock at t_2, the difference between c and D_0 resembles the profit of the investor.

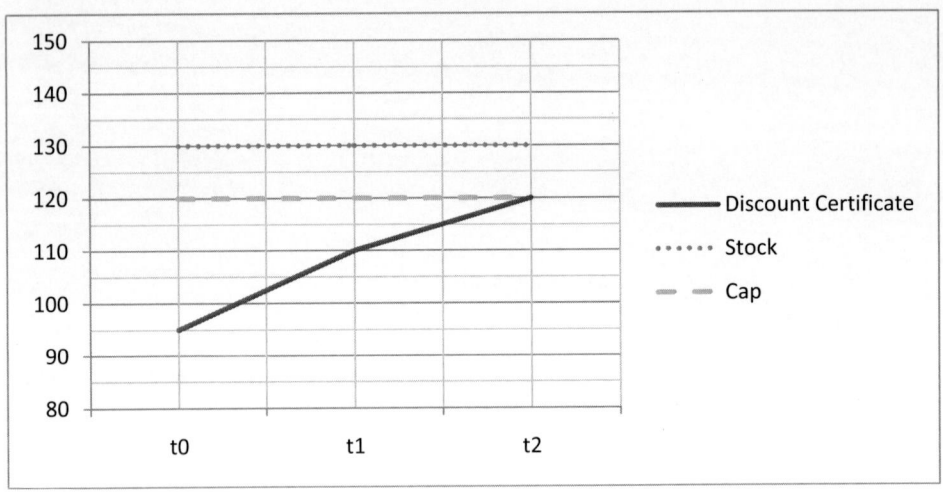

Figure 5: Stagnation II

In this scenario the investor can realize the complete expected profit (c – D_0).

Table 6: Payout Stagnation II

	Initial investment	payout	profit
DC	95	120	25 (26.3%)
stock	130	130	0 (0%)

In a stagnation scenario the DC investor will always make a profit while the stock investor does not.

In consequence, expecting a stagnating development of stock prices DCs are the investment of choice.

4.2.4 The Moderate Decline Scenarios

In the fourth scenario the value of the stock declines. This decline in is moderate, the value of the stock will not drop beneath the initial value of the DC at t_0. For the moderate decline scenario there are two possible situations at t_2.

In the first scenario the investor has bought a DC with "deep discount" (see also chapter 5.1).

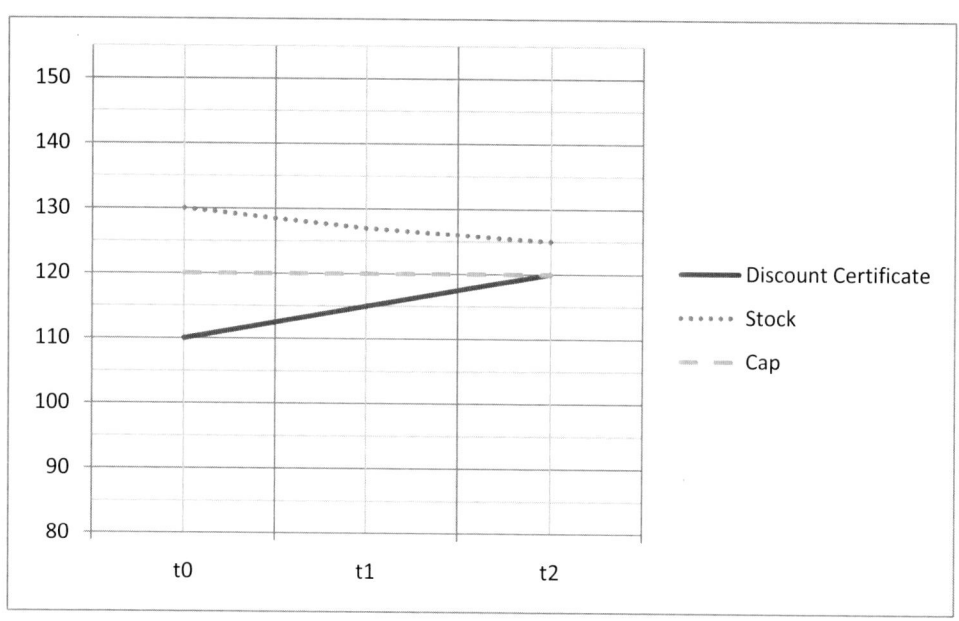

Figure 6: Moderate Decline I

As a consequence the initial stock price is listed above the cap of the DC. In this case, a moderate decline of the price of the underlying results in a stock value at t_2 which is above the cap. The DC investor is able to realize the complete profit margin of the DC (c- D_0). The stock investor will have realized a loss.

Table 7: Payout Moderate Decline I

	Initial investment	payout	profit
DC	95	120	25 (26.3%)
stock	130	125	-5 (-3.9%)

In the second scenario the price of the underlying at t_2 lists below the cap of the DC but above of D_0. In this example, $S_2 = 118$.

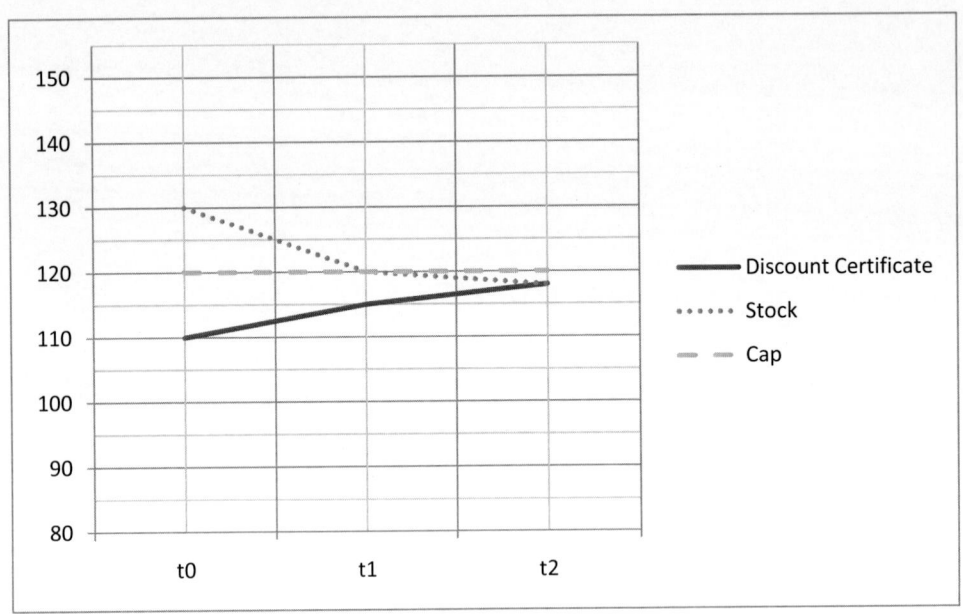

Figure 7: Moderate Decline II

In this case the DC investor makes a profit according to the difference in value between D_0 and the S_2. The stock investor will have made a loss.

Table 8: Payout Moderate Decline II

	Initial investment	payout	profit
DC	95	118	23 (24.2%)
stock	130	118	-12 (-9.2%)

For an investor, not eliminating the possibility of a loss in value of the underlying stock, the DC provides the security of generating a profit, even if the underlying decreases in value.

4.2.5 The Decline Scenario

The last scenario describes a strong decline of the underlying stock.
The difference to the scenario of moderate stock price declines lies in the fact that the value of the stock price decreases below the initial price of the DC.

The cap does not affect the profitability of the investment, because it is never reached by the DC. So the discount is the only variable having an impact in the outcome of the DC investment compared to the stock investment.

To visualize the fact, that the cap can be completely neglected in this scenario the values of the variables are changed. The initial value of the stock is 125 (S_0) and the discount is 15 (d). The cap stays the same at 120. In the example the stock drops to 95 during t_2-t_0.

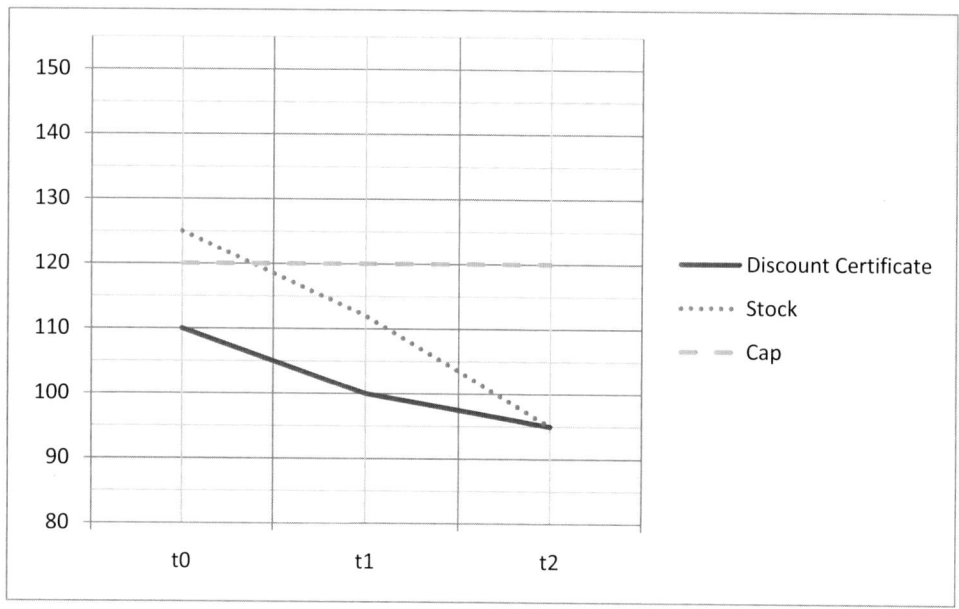

Figure 8: Decline

As figure 8 shows the investor makes a profit neither with a stock investment nor the investment into a DC. If expecting such a market scenario a rational investor will not invest into any of the two possibilities.

However, in reality market developments as the above can unexpectedly occur e.g. due to a crash of the financial markets.

Regardless of the type of investment the investor will realize a loss at t_2. The loss when invested into stocks, however, will be higher than a DC investment.

Table 9: Payout Decline

	Initial investment	payout	profit
DC	110	95	-15 (-13.6%)
stock	125	95	-30 (-24%)

During a sharp decline in the price of the underlying, the discount acts like a buffer against high losses.

Yet, this advantage is reduced the further the value of the stock drops. At the point of the stock value being zero at t_2, the value of the DC will also be zero. Although this results in a total loss for both investments, the DC will have lost less money in absolute numbers due to the initial discount.

4.3 Special considerations when investing in discount certificates

The value of a DC is not only determined by the development of the underlying stock. It is influenced by behavior of the option-component (short call), which is affected by volatility and maturity. The zero-strike-call is influenced by the expected dividends paid by the respective company and the maturity.

Implicit Volatility describes the uncertainty about future stock price movements (Hull 2003). For an investor in DCs who wants to hold the derivative until it matures, the volatility of the underlying is of minor interest. The payout of the DC is determined by the value of the underlying at the point of maturity. Changes of value prior to this point in time do not influence the payout of a DC at all. There are two ways the payout can occur, either the investor is paid out in cash or he receives the stock (details see Chapter 2.1).

However, for an investor who considers selling the DC before maturity, the volatility of the underlying is a major point of interest. The issuer of a DC has sold a call option. The person invested into a DC has hence also sold a call option on the underlying (short).

Therefore the volatility of the underlying will influence the value of a DC. The investor will profit from a decrease of volatility of the underlying in the course of maturity since the value of the DC increases when volatility decreases.

However this mechanism works in both directions. A DC will lose value if the volatility of the underlying increases. The influence of volatility on the value of the DC increases the closer the value of the DC is located at its cap. (Goldman Sachs 2008 p. 43, 35, and 45)

An investor can use this circumstance to bet on a decrease of volatility of the underlying, for details see Chapter 5.

A change in the expected dividends paid by the company has a direct influence on the value of the zero-strike-call. If more dividends are paid, the value decreases and vice versa. However, at the time of maturity the value of the DC equals either the cap or the stock value.

The investor has also to consider the maturity element when investing into a DC. The shorter the time for a DC to mature the higher the increase of value will be (Goldman Sachs 2008 p. 45). This increase is based on the construction of the DC. The zero-strike-call increase in value, since the dividends are paid and the zero-strike-call nears itself to the value of the underlying stock. In addition, the value of the call-option decreases (time value). This also increases the value of the DC. The DC investor is short on this call-option; therefore its decline in value increases the value of the DC.

4.4 Evaluation and Critical Review

Chapter 4.2 shows that DCs are superior to direct stock investments in virtually every market scenario. Now, one may argue that the assumptions made in Chapter 4.1 favor DCs since the payment of dividends is neglected. However, the payment of dividends can be neglected if a payment of dividends does not happen within the maturity of the DC (e. g. short-time investments). In addition, the expected dividends paid are already incorporated into the value of the DC (Chapter 2.1)

It is true that in a long-time-scenario dividends must be taken into consideration. Stocks will outperform DCs in any market environment, if the dividends paid exceed the discount. In reality, this happens most probable in growth and moderate growth scenarios. During a decline or moderate decline the it is rather improbable that the company pays more dividends than the investors have expected. Therefore Chapter 4.3 deals separately with the influence of dividends on DCs.

The assumption that the investor holds both investment types for the same time period has to be made in order to make the investments comparable. If one takes buy and sells of the investment types during t2-t0 in to account, timing and transactions cost weaken the comparability. The Element of maturity and volatility influence the DC more significantly than the stock, therefore they have been separately evaluated in chapter 4.3.

5 Strategies for investing into Discount Certificates

5.1 Classic Strategies

There are different portfolio strategies for investing in DCs. These strategies can be split into classic strategies and special strategies.

Issuers of DC commonly explain the classic strategies in their sales brochures. The classic strategies differ in terms of the location of the cap to value of the underlying stock at the time of purchase. They are long-time-strategies and assume that the investor buys the DC at the time of the initial offering and keeps the DC until it matures.

Doll (2009) distinguishes the following three types of classic strategies when investing in DCs:

- The defensive strategy
- The neutral strategy
- The offensive strategy

The defensive strategy is also called the "deep-discount-strategy". An investor who pursues a defensive strategy buys a DC with a cap below the current value of the underlying. The basic idea of this strategy is to avoid a loss even if the underlying drops in value (Jordan 2006).

The following calculation shows the principle of the deep-discount-strategy.

The price of a DC is 35, its cap is 40 and the value of the underlying is 65 at the time of purchase. Taking this in consideration the investor will make a profit as long as the underlying does not drop to 35 (a loss of 42%). In addition the investor will make a profit of 5 (14%) in any scenario in which the underlying does not lose more than 25 (a loss of 38%). This strategy is useful as an alternative to a savings account, since it provides much security. However, a high profit cannot be obtained by following this strategy, since the cap is chosen to low compared to the value of the stock.

If expecting a lateral movement of the underlying. The most profitable strategy for an investor is the neutral strategy. In this scenario the investor buys a DC "at the money". The cap of such a discount certificate locates at the price of the underlying. The investor makes a profit as long as the underlying does not drop beneath the initial price of the DC. It will outperform a stock investment if the price of the underlying does not rise or drop sharply (Linder 2006). This is a strategy for the stagnations scenario and the moderate growth/loss scenario (chapter 4.1).

An investor expecting a rise in the price of the underlying may use the offensive strategy. In this case, the cap of the DC locates above the current value of the underlying stock, while the discount is rather small. In this scenario the DC behaves almost like a stock investment. The investor will participate in losses of the underlying stock but receives in return an almost infinite participation of the gains of the underlying stock. The discount represents the more in profit compared to the stock investment. This strategy enables an investor to obtain a stock with a discount, if he does not expect the underlying to exceed the cap at the time of maturity of the DC. However, the investor must always keep in mind, that a DC does not pay dividends. In the long run the dividends paid by the company may be greater than the discount.
As a result an investor should this strategy if the DC has a short maturity (Chapter 5.2), because in the long run the direct stock invest is more profitable.

5.2 Unconventional Strategies

The unconventional strategies use the unique characteristics of a DC in order to outperform the direct stock investment. An investor can combine them with the classic strategies reducing the special risks implied in DC. Special strategies have a short time horizon of investment. They are usually not stated or not directly stated in the sales brochures of the issuers.

5.2.1 The short maturity strategy

The short maturity strategy describes the plan of investing into DC which matures within less than six month. The investor buys the DC at this point and holds on to it until maturity.

The basic idea of this strategy is to avoid the special risks of DCs and to outperform a stock investment by taking advantage of the increased performance of a DC at the end of maturity.

The first advantage of the short maturity strategy is to avoid the pricing risk of DCs (Chapter 3.2). The investor is likely to receive more favorable prices at the end of maturity of the DC, which increases the profit of the investment. In Addition the investor is able to reduce the issuer's risk of default. The smaller the time span until the DC matures, the smaller the likeliness that the issuing institute is not able to pay the investor. He is also able to anticipate the market development more accurate so that the risks implied by the underlying are reduced as well.

But the short maturity strategy does not only reduce the risk for the investor, it also enables him to take advantage of the increased gain in value of DC at the end of maturity (Chapter 2.1). The increase of the DC becomes significantly stronger that the increase of the underlying stock.

The short maturity strategy provides the investor with an increased certainty about the payout scenario. It also enables the investor to respond more flexible to market changes, since the capital invested is not tied up for a long period of time.

The short maturity strategy can be linked to the classic strategies. This linkage combines the advantages of the short maturity and with the purposes of the classical strategies.

5.2.1.1 The short maturity strategy combined with the offensive investment strategy

This combination allows an investor to purchase a particular stock for with a discount. This may be an interesting investment strategy for investors, who want to buy as many stocks of a certain company with a fixed amount of money. However this strategy needs to high volumes in order to translate the discount into a higher number of stocks purchased. The discount achievable maybe of such a small value, that it is not superior to a direct stock investment.

5.2.1.2 The short maturity strategy combined with the neutral strategy

Combining the short maturity strategy with the neutral strategy enables the investor to realize a considerable high profit in a short period of time. With this combination the investor is able to blend the advantages of the short maturity strategy with a classical strategy in a way which provides a high profit and low risk. The following example illustrates this fact:

Price of the stock	Price of the DC	Cap	Buffer[2] in %	Profit Margin[3] in %	DC matures in … days
41.86	38.58	42.00	8.5	8.8	97

Considering this the profit per annum calculates as the following:

(Profit Margin/Days to maturity)*365

(8.8/97)*365= 33.1% p.a.

So an investor will be able to realize 33.1% while holding the DC only for 97 days. This time span is easier to oversee than a year or longer. The investor is able to judge the development of the stock within this time period more precisely reducing the risk involved. In Addition, the money is only tied up for 97 days allowing the relocate it more quickly in comparison to a long time investment.

5.2.1.3 The short maturity strategy combined with the defensive strategy

Although the combination of the short maturity strategy with the defensive or deep discount strategy provides for high security, it does not allow the investor to make a big profit. The margins of this strategy are not very high. If the investor uses this strategy the margin may be as small as 0.01 of the respective currency. With margins so small, the investor may need a high volume of discount certificates in order to provide for a profit. As a result, the investor has to bind a considerable amount of

---
[2] Price of Stock divided by Price of DC
[3] Cap divided by Price of DC

money in this investment, which cannot be used for other investments. This makes this combination rather unattractive.

5.2.2 The low volatility strategy

This strategy derives from fact that the value of a DC increases with the decrease of the volatility of the underlying stock and vice versa. The investor can now use this fact for a volatility based strategy.

The investor will buy DC when the volatility of the underlying stock is high and sell it, when the volatility decreases. Thereby he uses the value change in the element of the call-option of the DC. However, this strategy very risky, since the value of the DC is also determined by the performance of the underlying stock. If the value of the underlying decreases this may offset the increase in value due to the reduced volatility of the underlying stock.

This strategy can improve profits, if a gain in value and a decrease of volatility of the underlying stock follows times of high volatility.

6 Conclusion

Discount Certificates are an alternative to stock investments, if the investor knows about the additional risks contained in investing into discount certificates. Chapter 4, however, has shown that discount certificates outperform stock investments in virtually any market scenario. Especially in uncertain or negative market environments discount certificates perform better than the underlying stock. Stock investments are inferior to discount certificates if the increase in value of the underlying is not significantly strong. However, discount certificates are not the holy grail of investment possibilities, since they expose the investor to additional risks (identified in chapter 3.1).

When investing into DCs one should always be aware of the "ingredients" of discount certificates. On the one hand they may work for an investor, especially when using the unconventional strategies explained in chapter 5.2. On the other they may be a disadvantage, especially if the investors is ignorant about them and makes therefore "bad" investment decisions.

Although this work offers interesting views of possible unconventional investment strategies for discount certificates. It shows that additional practical research, especially about the usefulness and profitability of the unconventional strategies has to be undertaken.

REFERENCE LIST

Alexander, C., & Sheedy, E. (2008). *The professional risk managers' guide to financial markets.* New York, NY: McGraw-Hill.

Baule, R., Entrop, O., & Wilkens, M. (2008). Credit Risk and Bank Margins in Structured Financial Products: Evidence from the German Secondary Market for Discount Certificates. *Journal of Futures Markets, 28*(4), 376–397. Retrieved March 02, 2010, from http://www-edit.ku-eichstaett.de/ Fakultaeten/WWF/Lehrstuehle/LFB/download/HF_sections/content/sfp_credit_risk_baule_entrop_wilkens.pdf.

Boerse Stuttgart AG (2010). Discount Finder [Internet]. Stuttgart: Boerse Stuttgart AG. Retrieved February 22, 2010, from https://www.boerse-stuttgart.de/rd/de/finder/discount/?suche=1&produktname_code=2&wp_keyword=&fnd_typ=aktien&submitform=Suchen.

Brechmann, A., Röder, J., Schneider, S., & Winkler, D. (2008). *Erfolgsweg Zertifikate: Strukturierte Produkte in der Beratungspraxis.* Wiesbaden: Gabler.

Commerzbank AG (2009). *Basisprospekt: Discount-Zertifikate bezogen auf Aktien.* Retrieved February 20, 2010, from Commerzbank AG: http://portal.commerzbank.de/cocoon/retail/SiteContent/1/1/1/148/676/736/056EURAktienDisco.pdf.

Doll, G. F. (2009). *Aktien-Zertifikate: Anlagestrategien, Gewinnprofile, Zusammenhänge.* Wiesbaden: Gabler.

Federal Reserve Bank of Atlanta (2009). *Spending and Credit.* Retrieved February 20, 2010, from Federal Reserve Bank of Atlanta: http://www.frbatlanta.org/edresources/personalfined/glossaries/spending_credit.cfm?redirected=true.

Goldman Sachs (2008). *Discount-Kompass.* Frankfurt am Main: Goldman Sachs International.

Hull, J. C. (2003). *Options, futures, & other derivatives.* Upper Saddle River, NJ: Prentice-Hall International.

Jordan, M. (2006). *Zertifikate: Rendite kalkulierbar machen; Leitfaden für eine moderne Geldanlage.* München: FinanzBuch-Verl.

Kolb, R. W., & Overdahl, J. A. (2003). *Financial derivatives.* New York: John Wiley.

Linder, M. (2006). *Discountzertifikate können Anlagestrategie optimieren.* Retrieved February 27, 2010, from Verlagsgruppe Handelsblatt GmbH (VHB): http://www.handelsblatt.com/finanzen/anlagestrategie/was-man-bei-discountzertifikaten-beachten-sollte;932276.

London Stock Exchange plc. (2008). *Lehman Brothers International (Europe) Default.* Retrieved February 28, 2010, from London Stock Exchange plc.: http://www.londonstockexchange.com/traders-and-brokers/rules-regulations/default-information/lehman-brothers/lehman-brothers-default.htm.

Maaß, C. (2007). *Discount-Zertifikate.* Frankfurt am Main: Sal. Oppenheim jr. &Cie. KGaA.

Mohr, D. (2008). *Zertifikate droht Totalausfall.* Retrieved February 20, 2010, from F.A.Z. Electronic Media GmbH: http://www.faz.net/s/Rub645F7F43865344D198A672E313F3D2C3/Doc~ED500DA444ECC4F679E42E8D97D2A32E8~ATpl~Ecommon~Sspezial.html.

Organisation for Economic Co-operation and Development [OECD] (2005). *Advances in risk management of government debt.* Paris: OECD Publ.

Schmidt, K. (2008). *Emittentenporträt: HSBC Trinkaus.* Retrieved February 19, 2010, from dasinvestment.com: http://www.dasinvestment.com/investments/zertifikate/news/datum/2008/02/01/emittentenportraet-hsbc-trinkaus/.

Wilkens, S., Erner, C., & Röder, K. (2003). *The Pricing of Structured Products: An Empirical Investigation of the German Market.* Münster: University of Münster - Chair of Finance (Münster). Retrieved March 01, 2010, from http://www.cofar.uni-mainz.de/dgf2003/paper/paper88.pdf.